iGCSE & GCSE ESSAY WRITING GUIDE - J.B. PRIESTLEY'S *AN INSPECTOR CALLS*

by Joe Broadfoot

All rights reserved

Copyright © Joe Broadfoot, 2014

The right of Joe Broadfoot to be identified as the author of this work has been asserted in accordance with Section 77 of the Copyright, Designs and Patents Act 1988

Brief Introduction

This book is aimed at iGCSE and GCSE students of English Literature who are studying J.B. Priestley's *An Inspector Calls*. The focus is on what examiners are looking for and here you will find relevant themes covered in detail. I hope this will help you and be a valuable tool in your studies and revision.

Criteria for high marks

Make sure you use appropriate critical language (see glossary of literary terms at the back). You need your argument to be fluent, well-structured and coherent. Stay focused!

Analyse and explore the use of form, structure and the language. Explore how these aspects affect the meaning.

Make connections between texts and look at different interpretations. Explore their strengths and weaknesses. Don't forget to use supporting references to strengthen your argument.

Analyse and explore the context.

Best essay practice

Use PEE for your paragraphs: point/evidence/explain.

Other tips

Make your studies active!

Don't just sit there reading! Never forget to annotate, annotate and annotate!

An Inspector Calls

iGCSE

J.B. Priestley's text is not necessarily one you'll encounter if you're doing iGCSE. However, I've noticed that it's recently become a popular choice of teachers, who are looking for something to engage students. *An Inspector Calls* generally does that and it also gives us plenty to debate, which may be why it is now being used for iGCSE coursework. Assignment 3 of the iGCSE course gives students a chance to write in response to an opinion. If you're going to do that, you need to write in a different format to most essays. Instead of being objective, as you should be in most academic essays, you should be subjective. In other words, you have to write in an opinionated way, using lines like: 'In my opinion'. Most students are good at that! Just don't make it a habit, as you should never forget that writing an iGCSE essay involves different skills to what you need with other exam boards.

If you're set an essay to complete for assignment 3 of your iGCSE coursework, the chances are it will be about notions of **collective responsibility** or **social responsibility**, which amounts to the same thing. I've seen questions that ask how Priestley's dramatises the words above (in bold) and, in answer to that question, the first thing I would do is draw four lines on a page, with the following sub-titles:

Evidence	Character's POV	JBP's POV	My POV

Then I would proceed to add notes beneath those sub-headings. For iGCSE, it is expected that students write between 8-10 paragraphs and between 500 and 800 words. Therefore I would be looking for at least 8 paragraph headings (which I would use for my initial notes, but delete when submitting the first draft). I would usually write more than that to start with and then cut out unnecessary or redundant sentences and phrases afterwards. You have to be ruthless with your editing: if you don't need something, cut it out!

The most common errors I've seen could mostly have been avoided. They come about because of students not proof-reading their work. Even the most intelligent ones are nbot immune, sometimes forgetting how to spell the playwright's name. Attention to detail is important. We all make mistakes, but please do your utmost to avoid them; it can make you look sloppy and send out all the wrong messages to the examiner, whom you want to impress.

Anyway, enough about that! Let's see how I would fare with the same question on social responsibility. I'll start with my notes.

Evidence	Character's	JBP's POV	My POV

	POV		
1. 'There's a good deal of silly talk about […] I speak as a hard-headed business man […] ignore all this silly pessimistic talk'	AB is interested in business & money only. Portrayed as wealthy, without much concern for employees. Lacks a social conscience	Doesn't agree with Arthur Birling. Shows it through dramatic irony when Birling predicts a prosperous & peaceful future, before Great Depression & WW1. JBP's arguing in favour of collective responsibility	In my opinion, rich business people can become obsessed with making profit to the detriment of their workers. OR I think rich business pay a lot of taxes etc
2. 'Just because the miners came out on strike…we employers are coming	AB is optimistic about the future. He believes that rich capitalists	Doesn't agree with AB. He makes him look ridiculous, as the General Strike of	Strikes do not appear to achieve very much, in my opinion. Many of the workers that

together...we're in for a time of steadily increasing prosperity'	will prevail over their poorer workforce	1926 and the Great Depression that followed proved AB's predictions were wrong	went out on strike in 1926 lost their jobs thereafter or took a cut in wages and worked longer hours. No wonder there hasn't been a general strike since
3. 'the Titanic...every luxury and unsinkable, absolutely unsinkable'	AB's blind belief in progress is exemplified by this quotation. He believes in what he reads in the newspapers	The Titanic's spectacular demise may be symbolic, as it shows how foolhardy people in power can be. The captain of the ill-fated ship shouted 'Every man for himself', according to	I believe belief has to be grounded in facts. It is always good to be sceptical of new developments

		some accounts after his ship hit an iceberg. He was an upwardly mobile middle-class man, like AB. Smith was known as the 'millionaire's captain'	
4. 'let's say in 1940 – by that time you'll be living in a world that will have forgotten all about these Capital versus Labour agitations'	AB is convinced that future strife will be averted, when it comes to industrial disputes	As a committed socialist, clearly JBP would disagree	Although there haven't been any general strikes, there have been many industrial disputes since 1926, some of which have nearly brought the country to a

			standstill. It seems that some irresponsible business owners will always put profits before the welfare of their workers and this bound to lead to industrial action.
5. 'a man has to make his own way – has to look after himself – and his family too...these cranks talk...everybody has to look after everybody else (like) bees in a hive –	AB believes a man should look after his family, but put himself first. He's a social Darwinist.	Rather than believing in 'survival of the fittest', JBP wanted to promote a more egalitarian and fairer society.	While family is important, equality is important. If we followed AB's example the business world would be even more riddled with nepotism than it is.

community and all that nonsense			
6. 'I have an idea that your [Gerald's] mother - Lady Croft - while she doesn't object to my girl [Sheila] - feels you might have done better for yourself socially'	AB is feeling the effects of being nouveau riche as opposed to being born 'with a silver spoon in his mouth'	JBP is making the audience realise that even the prejudiced suffer discrimination sometimes	I think the class system still exists in British society and, although there is more upward and downward mobility nowadays, unfortunately prejudice on the basis of class is still with us
7. 'We can't let all these Bernard Shaws and H.G. Wellses do all the talking'	AB is attacking two prominent literary socialists	JBP is making the political battle lines clearer to the audience	We should listen to both sides of an argument before making our minds up, but AB's blustering

			form of conservatism is utterly unconvincing
8. 'They'll be peace and prosperity everywhere - except of course in Russia - which will always be behindhand, naturally'	AB's xenophobia and racism is apparent	JBP portrays AB as a bigot, whom it is almost impossible for the audience to sympathise with.	Xenophobia and racism are completely irrational. The only way to bring peace and prosperity to the world is by the elimination of negativity.

Now that I've come up with 8 quotations, I'm going to turn this into my first essay draft (without an introduction or a conclusion). Note that I won't start any paragraph with a quotation and I may well break them up into more manageable chunks.

1st draft

Paragraph 1 - hard-headed businessman?

Arthur Birling is interested in business and money mainly. He's portrayed as wealthy, without much concern for employees. He also seems to lacks a social conscience, but admits it, as he describes himself as 'a hard-headed businessman'. He is the eternal optimist, telling anyone who will listen to 'ignore all this silly pessimistic talk'. However, with World War One looming on the horizon in 1912 (when the play is set), there is a lot to be pessimistic about. Priestley is using dramatic irony to portray Birling as a buffoon and discredit his opinions. While it is difficult to condemn someone for being an optimist, it is not good to have a dreamer masquerading as a realist, as appears to be the case with Birling. In short, he is the type of character that gives business a bad name, as he's dim-witted rather than 'hard-headed'.

Paragraph 2 - miners

Indeed, Birling's predictions are continually lampooned through the use of dramatic irony. The audience has the benefit of hindsight and knows the error inherent in other Birling statements, such as: 'Just because the miners came out on strike, there's a lot of wild talk about possible labour trouble'. Priestley deliberately makes sure that Birling 'gets egg on his face', as most of the audience will know the General Strike of 1926 brought the country to a standstill just over a decade later. However, the strikers were not victorious ultimately, as many lost their jobs in the aftermath, or had to suffer longer hours or pay cuts. As much as Birling is ridiculed by the playwright, it is usually the business owners who win industrial disputes.

Paragraph 3 - Titanic

Although not quite as much a victim as impoverished pre-World War One workers, Birling is also a dupe. His blind belief in progress and the mass media is exemplified by his description of the Titanic as 'absolutely unsinkable'. No doubt many people in 1912 believed this to be true, shortly before the boat sank in April of that year. Priestley is showing how what the majority believe is not necessarily the truth and that we should question everything. It represents the failings of big business, who put profits before the safety of passengers. This, of course, led to a catastrophic loss of life when the doomed ship hit an iceberg as there were not enough lifeboats on board. Like Priestley, I believe that all lives are worth protecting, no matter what the cost.

Paragraph 4 - Social Darwinism

Interestingly, the captain of the aforementioned Titanic, Edward Smith, may have agreed with Birling on many issues, given his last words were reputed to be: 'every man for himself'. This sentiment is echoed in the play by Birling, who says: 'a man [...] has to look after himself – and his family too'. Birling believes in survival of the fittest, economically at least, judging by this quotation and his lack of sympathy for the plight of Eva Smith, later in the play. As a committed socialist, Priestley would have frowned on this type of individualism or Social Darwinism. Likewise, while I believe individuals must look after themselves, I don't think it should be to the detriment of others.

Paragraph 5 - social prejudice

Ironically, Birling himself is the victim of a similar kind of sentiment. While he has married into the upper classes, his offspring, Sheila, is still not considered the equal of Gerald Croft. Birling shows he is aware of the social disparity, when he says to Gerald: 'I have an idea that your mother - Lady Croft - while she doesn't object to my girl - feels you might have done better for yourself socially'. Priestley may not quite make the audience sympathise with Birling's character at this point, but at least the playwright shows us that even the prejudiced can be victims of discrimination. While that does not justify discriminatory behaviour, it makes one realise how class warfare can be perpetuated: Birling's desperation to be accepted by the aristocracy may have led to him distancing himself from the working classes.

Paragraph 6 - racism

Another form of prejudice rears its ugly head in the play, when Birling speaks of Russia. He clearly underestimates that nation's capabilities as he refers to them as 'behindhand, naturally'. He also prefaces that, by saying they will 'always' be that way. Birling is suggesting that Russia will be perpetually backward, and such a statement smacks of racism and xenophobia. Ironically, despite his belief in 'peace and prosperity' in years to come, attitudes like these can lead to warfare. Priestley shows the audience that Birling's prejudice knows no bounds, which makes him a truly unsympathetic character. If we want to make the world a safer and better place to live, we have to try eliminate all forms of prejudice from our hearts and minds.

Paragraph 7 - sexual discrimination

However, another form of prejudice exists within Birling, which manifests itself in the form of sexual discrimination. He tells Sheila that when she's married she'll 'realize that men with important work to do sometime have to spend nearly all their time and energy on business'. Ironically, Gerald, her fiancé, had been spending much of the last summer being unfaithful. Birling's words later take on a new resonance, as 'important work' becomes a euphemism for 'an affair'. Priestley, once again, makes the audience despise Birling's attitude; although Gerald's infidelity is yet to be revealed, at this stage. Although Birling also tells his daughter that she'll have to get used to it, her reply that she doesn't 'believe' she 'will' indicates her resistance to the dominant patriarchy. While I would commend her behaviour by 1912 standards, I would expect her to be much more outspoken in the face of sexual discrimination if it were to happen in a modern setting.

Paragraph 8 - ageism

Birling's condescending and patronising tone is not simply reserved for women: his children are also victims in that sense. The fact that he talks over them indicates he doesn't listen to their views. When Eric tries to speak early on in the play, Birling continues in the same dominant vein, telling him:

'You've a lot to learn yet'. Priestley later shows us the irony in that statement, as it's Birling and his wife who learn the least after the Inspector's call. Priestley belief that younger people have more capability to learn from their mistakes than older people is exemplified by the older Birlings comparative lack of remorse at the end of the play. Of course, I would like to see the next generation make less mistakes than the previous one, but I'm not sure that will happen unless we work hard to make sure it does.

Comments

Right then. I've completed the main body of the text, adding a couple of quotation that didn't feature in my plan. I just wanted the piece to flow and once I started writing about prejudice I ran with it. That made for clear paragraph headings, making it easier for me to switch gently from subject to subject. However, it's 1,125 words long. Oh no! A lot of editing needs to be done. Obviously, I'm going to get rid of the sub-titles, but I'm going to have to be ruthless. Let's go editing!

2nd draft

Arthur Birling seems to lack a social conscience, but admits it, as he describes himself as 'a hard-headed businessman'. He is the eternal optimist, telling anyone who will listen to 'ignore all this silly pessimistic talk'. However, with World War One looming on the horizon in 1912 (when the play is set), there is a lot of pessimism about. Priestley is using dramatic irony to portray Birling as a buffoon and discredit his opinions. In short, he is giving business a bad name, as he's dim-witted rather than 'hard-headed'.

Indeed, Birling's predictions are continually lampooned through the use of dramatic irony. The audience has the benefit of hindsight and know the error inherent in other Birling statements, such as: 'Just because the miners came out on strike, there's a lot of wild talk about possible labour trouble'. Priestley deliberately makes sure that Birling 'gets egg on his face', as most of the audience will know the General Strike of 1926 brought the country to a standstill just over a decade later. However, the strikers were not victorious ultimately, as many lost their jobs in the aftermath, or had to suffer longer hours or pay cuts. As much as Birling is ridiculed by the playwright, it is usually the business owners who win industrial disputes.

Although not quite as much a victim as impoverished pre-First World War workers, Birling is also a dupe. His blind belief in progress and the mass media is exemplified by his description of the Titanic as 'absolutely unsinkable'. For Priestley, it represents the failings of big business, who put profits before the safety of passengers. This, of course, led to a catastrophic loss of life when the doomed ship hit an iceberg as there were not enough lifeboats on board. Like Priestley, I believe that all lives are worth protecting, no matter what the cost.

Interestingly, the captain of the aforementioned Titanic, Edward Smith, may have agreed with Birling on many issues, given his last words were reputed to be: 'every man for himself'. This sentiment is echoed in the play by Birling, who says: 'a man [...] has to look after himself – and his family too'. Birling believes in survival of the fittest, economically at least, judging by this quotation. As a committed socialist, Priestley would have frowned on this type of individualism or Social Darwinism. Likewise, while I believe individuals must look after themselves, I don't think it should be to the detriment of others.

Ironically, Birling himself is the victim of a similar kind of sentiment. While he has married into the upper classes, his offspring, Sheila, is still not considered the equal of Gerald Croft. Birling's awareness of the social disparity is revealed, when he says to Gerald: 'I have an idea that your mother - Lady Croft - while she doesn't object to my girl - feels you might have done better for yourself socially'. Priestley may not quite make the audience sympathise with Birling's character at this point, but at least the playwright shows us that even the prejudiced can be victims of discrimination. While that does not justify discriminatory behaviour, it makes one realise how class warfare can be perpetuated: Birling's desperation to be accepted by the aristocracy may have led to him distancing himself from the working classes.

Another form of prejudice rears its ugly head in the play, when Birling speaks of Russia. He clearly underestimates that nation's capabilities as he refers to them as 'behindhand, naturally'. Priestley shows the audience that Birling's prejudice knows no bounds, which makes him a truly unsympathetic character. If we want to make the world a safer and better place to live, we have to try eliminate all forms of prejudice from our hearts and minds.

However, another form of prejudice exists within Birling, which manifests itself in the form of sexual discrimination. He tells Sheila that when she's married she'll 'realize that men with important work to do sometime have to spend nearly all their time and energy on business'. Ironically, Gerald, her fiancé, had been spending much of the last summer being unfaithful. Priestley, once again, makes the audience despise Birling's attitude; although Gerald's infidelity is yet to be revealed, at this stage. Although Birling also tells his daughter that she'll have to get used to it, her reply that she doesn't 'believe' she 'will' indicates her resistance to the dominant patriarchy. While I would commend her behaviour by 1912 standards, I would expect her to be much more outspoken in the face of sexual discrimination if it were to happen in a modern setting.

Birling's condescending and patronising tone is not simply reserved for women: his children are also victims in that sense. The fact that he talks over them indicates he doesn't listen to their views. When Eric tries to speak early on in the play, Birling continues in the same dominant vein, telling him: 'You've a lot to learn yet'. Priestley later shows us the irony in that statement, as it's Birling and his wife who learn the least after the Inspector's call. Priestley belief that younger people have more capability to learn from their mistakes than older people is exemplified by the older Birlings comparative lack of remorse at the end of the play. Of course, I would like to see the next generation make less mistakes than the previous one, but I'm not sure that will happen unless we work hard to make sure it does.

Comments

Drat! 912 words! All that painful cutting and I've still got more editing to do. Okay. Here's draft number 3.

3rd Draft

Birling lacks a social conscience, evidenced when he describes himself as 'a hard-headed businessman'. In short, Priestley allows Birling to give business a bad name, as he's dim-witted rather than 'hard-headed'. How could anyone respect Birling?

Indeed, Birling's predictions are continually lampooned through the use of dramatic irony. The audience has the benefit of hindsight and know the error inherent in other Birling statements, such as: 'Just because the miners came out on strike, there's a lot of wild talk about possible labour trouble'. Priestley and his audience knew of the General Strike of 1926. However, as much as Birling is ridiculed by the playwright, it is usually the business owners who win industrial disputes.

Like his prediction about future industrial unrest, Birling's belief in the Titanic's 'unsinkable' reputation is similarly misplaced. For Priestley, the ship represents the failings of big business, who put profits before the safety of passengers. Like Priestley, I believe that all lives are worth protecting, no matter what the cost.

Interestingly, the captain of the aforementioned Titanic, Edward Smith, may have agreed with Birling on many issues, given his last words were reputed to be: 'every man for himself'. This sentiment is echoed in the play by Birling, who says: 'a man [...] has to look after himself – and his family too'. As a committed socialist, Priestley would have frowned on this type of individualism or Social Darwinism. Likewise, while I believe individuals must look after themselves, I don't think it should be to the detriment of others.

Ironically, Birling himself is the victim of a similar kind of attitude. While he has married into the upper classes, his offspring, Sheila, is still not considered the equal of Gerald Croft. Birling says to Gerald: 'I have an idea that your mother - Lady Croft - while she doesn't object to my girl - feels you might have done better for yourself socially'. While Priestley may not quite make the audience sympathise with Birling's character at this point, at least the playwright shows us that even the prejudiced can be victims of discrimination. While that does not justify discriminatory behaviour, it makes one realise how class warfare can be perpetuated.

Another form of prejudice rears its ugly head in the play, when Birling speaks of Russia. He clearly underestimates that nation's capabilities, referring to them as 'behindhand, naturally'. Priestley shows the audience that Birling's prejudice knows no bounds, which makes him a truly unsympathetic character. If we want to make the world a safer and better place to live, we have to try eliminate all forms of prejudice from our hearts and minds.

However, another form of prejudice exists within Birling: sexual discrimination. He tells Sheila that when she's married she'll 'realize that men with important work to do sometime have to spend nearly all their time and energy on business'. Ironically, Gerald, her fiancé, had been spending much of the last summer being unfaithful. Priestley, once again, makes the audience despise Birling's attitude; although Gerald's infidelity is yet to be revealed, at this stage. Although Birling also tells his daughter that she'll have to get used to it, her reply that she doesn't 'believe' she 'will' indicates her resistance to the dominant patriarchy. While I would commend her behaviour by 1912 standards, I would expect her to be much more outspoken in the face of sexual discrimination if it were to happen in a modern setting.

Birling's condescending and patronising tone is not simply reserved for women: his children are also victims. When Eric tries to speak early on in the play, Birling continues to dominate, saying: 'You've a lot to learn yet'. Priestley later shows us the irony in that statement, as it's Birling and his wife who learn the least after the Inspector's call. Priestley's belief that younger people have more capability to learn from their mistakes than older people is exemplified by the older Birlings' comparative lack of remorse at the end of the play. Of course, I would like to see the next generation make less mistakes than the previous one, but I'm not sure that will happen unless we work hard to make sure it does.

Comments

Wow! Still found a few mistakes, which I corrected. That's why you've got to keep editing. The good news is I'm down to 696 words now. That means I can use a 100 words on an introduction and a conclusion, so let's have a crack at that. First of all, I need to bring back my sub-titles.

Paragraph 1 - hard-headed businessman?

Paragraph 2 - miners

Paragraph 3 - The Titanic

Paragraph 4 - Social Darwinism

Paragraph 5 - social prejudice

Paragraph 6 - racism

Paragraph 7 - sexual discrimination

Paragraph 8 - ageism

I will incorporate all the above into my introduction. Here it goes:

Introduction

Social attitudes are examined in detail by Priestley in the play, particularly through the character of Birling, who represents an archetypal 1912 businessman. His attitudes towards the miners, The Titanic, family, class, race, gender and the younger generation will be each be explored in that order.

Comments

I had to change some of the paragraph headings to make it work, as I was discussing Birling's attitudes. However, I'm really pleased to tell the examiner what's coming up in this essay in less than 50 words! Now I've got more than 50 left for a conclusion. Once again, let's look at our paragraph headings and this time try to add the briefest concluding word(s) next to each of them.

Paragraph 1 - hard-headed businessman? - dim-witted

Paragraph 2 - miners - owners win

Paragraph 3 - The Titanic - profits put first

Paragraph 4 - Social Darwinism - family first

Paragraph 5 - social prejudice - victim of class

Paragraph 6 - racism - abuser

Paragraph 7 - sexual discrimination - abuser

Paragraph 8 - ageism - abuser

Birling is representative of the world's social evils: he embodies and promotes ageism, sexual discrimination, racism and class prejudice - although, he is also the victim of the latter. The audience are taken on a trip through history and we see the results of these vile and dim-witted points of view: the loss of life and dignity.

Comments

I wanted to write more, but I've restrained myself. That's 57 words for my conclusion. I've now got around 800 words for my assignment 3 for iGCSE and I'm a happy bunny!

Am I addressing the question of social attitudes? I think so. How about you? Check your work again!

AQA Unit 1

If you're studying with AQA, there's a good chance your teachers will choose this text to study. There are good reasons for that: it's moralistic and it's popular with students. It may not be action-packed, but the text encourages us to think about right and wrong. It also makes us consider the boundaries of our responsibilities.

The text forms part of AQA's Section A. This section is supposed to be easier for students to access, as it's comprised purely of post-1945 texts. This provides students with a good grounding before they tackle Section B, which are arguably more challenging.

Anyway, here we will mostly focus on Section A and specifically what students need to look at when studying *An Inspector Calls* for an examination. As an AQA student, your focus needs to be on the following aspects:

1. ideas
2. themes and issues
3. characterisation

4. settings

But before we discuss those aspects, first of all, we will also look at a specific issue or theme that may be useful for your controlled assessment: the dramatisation of social attitudes.

Let's look at a few quotations from the text in note form and then convert those notes into PEE paragraphs.

Notes

Point 1: Birling is interested in business and money. Portrayed as wealthy, without much concern for employees. Lacks a social conscience.

Evidence/Quotation 1: 'There's a good deal of silly talk about […] I speak as a hard-headed business man […] ignore all this silly pessimistic talk'

Explanation 1: JBP doesn't agree with Arthur Birling. Shows it through dramatic irony when Birling predicts a prosperous & peaceful future, before Great Depression & WW1. JBP's arguing in favour of collective responsibility.

So that's what the notes look like. Let's convert those notes into a PEE paragraph.

Finished PEE paragraph

Birling seems interested in business and money mainly. He is generally portrayed as wealthy, without much concern for his employees. He appears to lack a social conscience and this is exemplified when he says: 'There's a good deal of silly talk about […] I speak as a hard-headed business man […] ignore all this silly pessimistic talk'. He seems proud of himself and it's clear that the playwright is setting Birling up for a fool to discredit Birling's views. J.B. Priestley does this effectively through the use of dramatic irony, as the 'pessimistic talk' that Birling refers to is quite accurate with the benefit of historical hindsight. The play is set just before World War One and the Great Depression that followed a decade or so afterwards. Additionally, the playwright makes Birling appear to be pompous and dismissive of other points of view, which the character describes as 'silly'. Priestley does not want his audience to sympathise with this character, who is a capitalist and would therefore be completely opposed to the playwright's brand of socialism and collective responsibility.

Okay, I'll be honest! I'm not expecting you to write that much for each quotation you use. By the way, 'quotation' is a noun and 'quote' is a verb. Some markers may be sticklers for accuracy, so I suggest you can quotations exactly that! Even if your teachers insists that anything that appears within quotation marks is a quote. If that were true, wouldn't they be called 'quote marks'! Forgive me, I digress!

What you should be writing for a PEE paragraph is a minimum of 3 sentences. I'd aim for about 4 or 5 generally, as you need to really explain the relevance of your quotation and refer back to the question to make sure you're on track. It's very easy to go off on a tangent, so by referring back to the question in the last sentence of each paragraph you can ensure that you stay on task.

Essay writing tips

Tip 1: Use a variety of connectives

Have a look of this list of connectives. Which of these would you choose to use?

'ADDING' DISCOURSE MARKERS

- AND
- ALSO
- AS WELL AS
- MOREOVER
- TOO
- FURTHERMORE
- ADDITIONALLY

I hope you chose 'additionally', 'furthermore' and 'moreover'. Don't be afraid to use the lesser discourse markers, as they are also useful. Just avoid using those ones over and over again. I've seen essays from Key Stage 4 students that use the same discourse marker for the opening sentence of each paragraph! Needless to say, those essays didn't get great marks!

Okay, here are some more connectives for you to look at. Select the best ones.

'SEQUENCING' DISCOURSE MARKERS

- NEXT
- FIRSTLY
- SECONDLY
- THIRDLY
- FINALLY
- MEANWHILE
- AFTER
- THEN
- SUBSEQUENTLY

This time, I hope you chose 'subsequently' and 'meanwhile'.

Here are some more connectives for you to 'grade'!

'ILLUSTRATING / EXEMPLIFYING' DISCOURSE MARKERS

- FOR EXAMPLE
- SUCH AS
- FOR INSTANCE
- IN THE CASE OF
- AS REVEALED BY
- ILLUSTRATED BY

I'd probably go for 'illustrated by' or even 'as exemplified by' (which is not in the list!). Please feel free to add your own examples to the lists. Strong connectives impress examiners. Don't forget it! That's why I want you to look at some more.

'CAUSE & EFFECT' DISCOURSE MARKERS

- BECAUSE
- SO
- THEREFORE
- THUS
- CONSEQUENTLY
- HENCE

I'm going for 'consequently' this time. How about you? What about the next batch?

'COMPARING' DISCOURSE MARKERS

- SIMILARLY
- LIKEWISE
- AS WITH
- LIKE
- EQUALLY
- IN THE SAME WAY

I'd choose 'similarly' this time. Still some more to go.

'QUALIFYING' DISCOURSE MARKERS

- BUT
- HOWEVER
- WHILE
- ALTHOUGH
- UNLESS
- EXCEPT
- APART FROM
- AS LONG AS

It's 'however' for me!

'CONTRASTING' DISCOURSE MARKERS

- WHEREAS
- INSTEAD OF
- ALTERNATIVELY
- OTHERWISE
- UNLIKE
- ON THE OTHER HAND

- CONVERSELY

I'll take 'conversely' or 'alternatively' this time.

'EMPHASISING' DISCOURSE MARKERS

- ABOVE ALL
- IN PARTICULAR
- ESPECIALLY
- SIGNIFICANTLY
- INDEED
- NOTABLY

You can breathe a sigh of relief now! It's over! No more connectives. However, now I want to put our new found skills to use in our essays. Here's my example of the use of connectives (in bold) with the **characterisation** of Birling in capital letters.

There are a number of examples of dramatic irony, which are mainly used to discredit characters' points of view. **Firstly,** Arthur Birling is spectacularly wrong about the future when he discusses the Titanic (p.7). **Therefore**, Birling appears to be ARROGANT, and OVER-CONFIDENT with an inner belief that HE'S ALWAYS RIGHT. **Although** those attributes can be useful to a hard-headed businessman whose sole interest is making profit, they do not make him a sympathetic character on stage. **Thus** ,it is clear that Priestley doesn't agree with Arthur

Birling. The playwright shows it through dramatic irony. Priestley portrays Birling as a ridiculous figure, who seems to believe that the Titanic epitomises progress in the capitalist world. Unlike the audience, Birling is unaware that the ship is about to sink, which effectively discredits all of his other points of view.

Now I'm going to give you a series of quotations that you should try to change into PEE paragraphs.

Other useful Birling quotations

'Just because the miners came out on strike […]we employers are coming together'

'we're in for a time of steadily increasing prosperity'

'the Titanic […]every luxury and unsinkable, absolutely unsinkable'

'let's say in 1940 – by that time you'll be living in a world that will have forgotten all about these Capital versus Labour agitations'

'a man has to make his own way – has to look after himself – and his family too[…]these cranks talk[…]everybody has to look after everybody else (like) bees in a hive – community and all that nonsense'

'Germans don't want war'

'Russia […]will always be behind'

'We can't let these Bernard Shaws and H.G. Wellses do all the talking'

'When you marry, you'll be marrying at a very good time'

Let's try to link those quotation to the playwright's beliefs, some of which you can see below.

Priestley's views

- He wants people to seize the chance the end of the World War Two has given them to build a better, more caring and responsible society

- He was a socialist

- He wanted people to develop a social conscience and embrace collective responsibility

- He is trying to show that upper classes are unaware that the easy lives they lead depend upon the hard work of the lower classes

- He is optimistic that the future generations will be better able to share and show more collective responsibility than their forefathers

Other useful quotations

'Oh I wish you hadn't told me' - Sheila, appearing to be a bit selfish

'All right. I knew her. Let's leave it at that' - Gerald, thinking he can hide his secret from Sheila

'I don't know really. Suddenly I just felt I had to laugh' - Eric, realising he has something to hide

'We've been had. That's all' - Birling, revealing he hasn't learned anything

'Go and look for the father of the child. It's his responsibility' - Sybil, trying to blame other people

'Your daughter isn't living on the moon. She's here in Brumley too' - The Inspector, thinking that Birling is patronising Sheila

Useful information/Glossary

Allegory: extended metaphor, like the grim reaper representing death, e.g. Scrooge symbolizing capitalism.

Alliteration: same consonant sound repeating, e.g. 'She sells sea shells'.

Allusion: reference to another text/person/place/event.

Ascending tricolon: sentence with three parts, each increasing in power, e.g. 'ringing, drumming, shouting'.

Aside: character speaking so some characters cannot hear what is being said. Sometimes, an aside is directly to the audience. It's a dramatic technique which reveals the character's inner thoughts and feelings.

Assonance: same vowel sounds repeating, e.g. 'Oh no, won't Joe go?'

Bathos: abrupt change from sublime to ridiculous for humorous effect.

Blank verse: lines of unrhymed iambic pentameter.

Compressed time: when the narrative is fast-forwarding through the action.

Descending tricolon: sentence with three parts, each decreasing in power, e.g. 'shouting, talking, whispering'.

Denouement: tying up loose ends, the resolution.

Diction: choice of words or vocabulary.

Dilated time: opposite compressed time, here the narrative is in slow motion.

Direct address: second person narrative, predominantly using the personal pronoun 'you'.

Dramatic action verb: manifests itself in physical action, e.g. I punched him in the face.

Dramatic irony: audience knows something that the character is unaware of.

Ellipsis: leaving out part of the story and allowing the reader to fill in the narrative gap.

End-stopped lines: poetic lines that end with punctuation.

Epistolary: letter or correspondence-driven narrative.

Flashback/Analepsis: going back in time to the past, interrupting the chronological sequence.

Flashforward/Prolepsis: going forward in time to the future, interrupting the chronological sequence.

Foreshadowing/Adumbrating: suggestion of plot developments that will occur later in the narrative.

Gothic: another strand of Romanticism, typically with a wild setting, a sensitive heroine, an older man with a 'piercing gaze', discontinuous structure, doppelgangers, guilt and the 'unspeakable' (according to Eve Kosofsky Sedgwick).

Hamartia: character flaw, leading to that character's downfall.

Hyperbole: exaggeration for effect.

Iambic pentameter: a line of ten syllables beginning with a lighter stress alternating with a heavier stress in its perfect form, which sounds like a heartbeat. The stress falls on the even syllables, numbers: 2, 4, 6, 8 and 10, e.g. 'When now I think you can behold such sights'.

Intertextuality: links to other literary texts.

Irony: amusing or cruel reversal of expected outcome or words meaning the opposite to their literal meaning.

Metafiction/Romantic irony: self-conscious exposure of the devices used to create 'the truth' within a work of fiction.

Motif: recurring image use of language or idea that connects the narrative together and creates a theme or mood, e.g. 'green light' in *The Great Gatsby.*

Oxymoron: contradictory terms combined, e.g. deafening silence.

Pastiche: imitation of another's work.

Pathetic fallacy: a form of personification whereby inanimate objects show human attributes, e.g. 'the sea smiled benignly'. The originator of the term, John Ruskin in 1856, used 'the cruel, crawling foam', from Kingsley's *The Sands of Dee*, as an example to clarify what he meant by the 'morbid' nature of pathetic fallacy.

Personification: concrete or abstract object made human, often simply achieved by using a capital letter or a personal pronoun, e.g. 'Nature', or describing a ship as 'she'.

Pun/Double entendre: a word with a double meaning, usually employed in witty wordplay but not always.

Retrospective: account of events after they have occurred.

Romanticism: genre celebrating the power of imagination, spriritualism and nature.

Semantic/lexical field: related words about a single concept, e.g. king, queen and prince are all concerned with royalty.

Soliloquy: character thinks aloud, but is not heard by other characters (unlike in a monologue) giving the audience access to inner thoughts and feelings.

Style: choice of language, form and structure, and effects produced.

Synecdoche: one part of something referring to the whole, e.g. Carker's teeth represent him in *Dombey and Son*.

Syntax: the way words and sentences are placed together.

Tetracolon climax: sentence with four parts, culminating with the last part, e.g. 'I have nothing to offer but blood, toil, tears, and sweat ' (Winston Churchill).

ABOUT THE AUTHOR

Joe Broadfoot is a secondary school teacher of English and a soccer journalist, who also writes fiction and literary criticism. His former experiences as a DJ took him to far-flung places such as Tokyo, Kobe, Beijing, Hong Kong, Jakarta, Cairo, Dubai, Cannes, Oslo, Bergen and Bodo. He is now PGCE and CELTA-qualified with QTS, a first-class honours degree in Literature and an MA in Victorian Studies. Drama is close to his heart as he acted in 'Macbeth' and 'A Midsummer Night's Dream' at the Royal Northern College of Music in Manchester. More recently, he has been teaching 'Much Ado About Nothing' to 'A' Level students at a secondary school in Buckinghamshire and 'An Inspector Calls' at a school in west London.

Printed in Great Britain
by Amazon.co.uk, Ltd.,
Marston Gate.